I Am Ann

By Carolyn Mc Carthy Illustrated by Bob Masheris

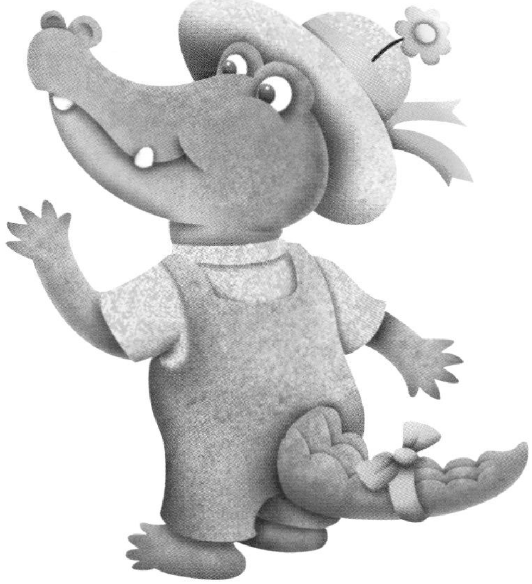

Target Skill Short *Aa*/*a*/

Scott Foresman
is an imprint of

PEARSON

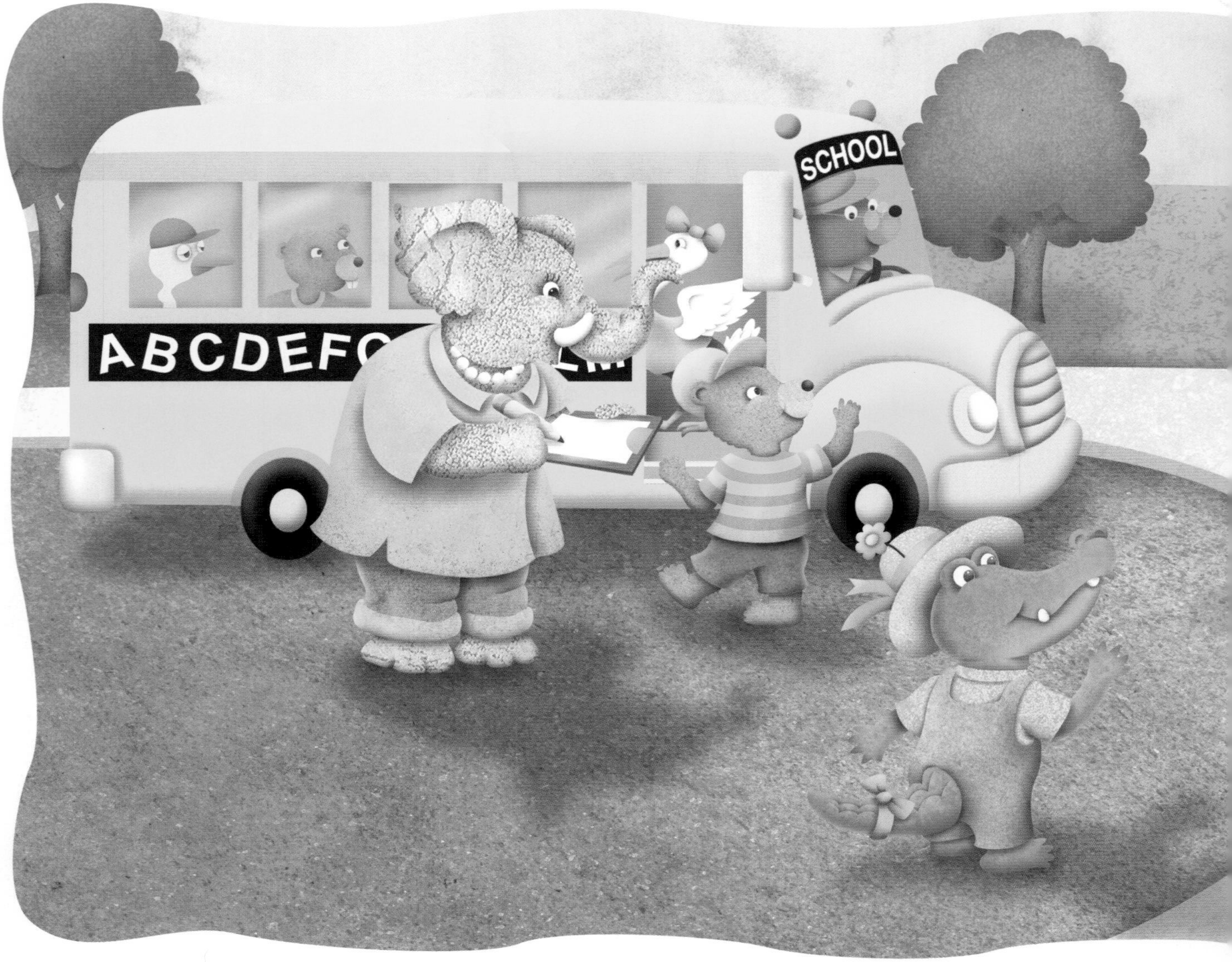

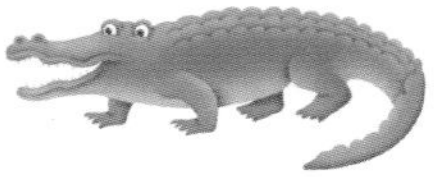

alligator

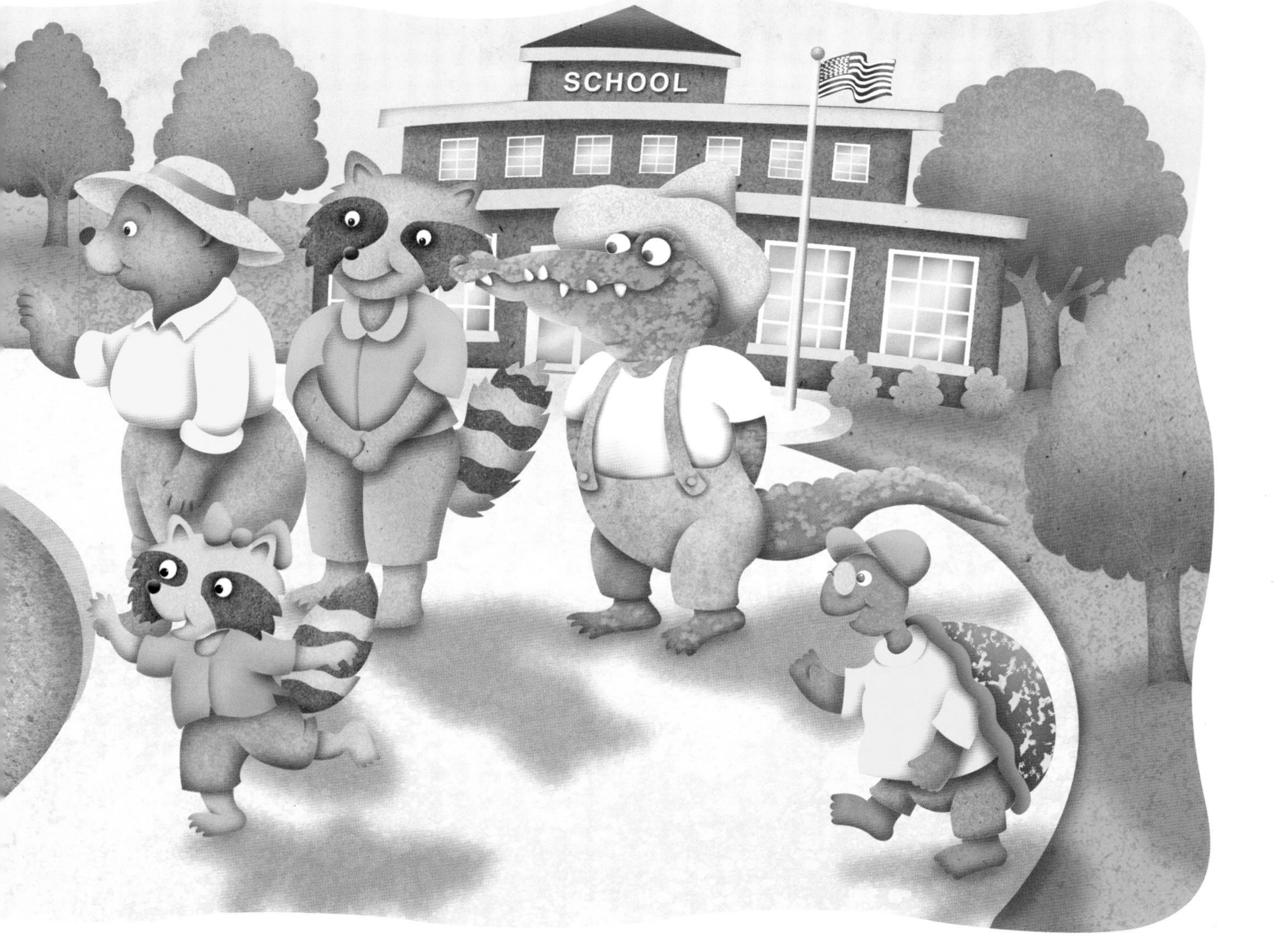

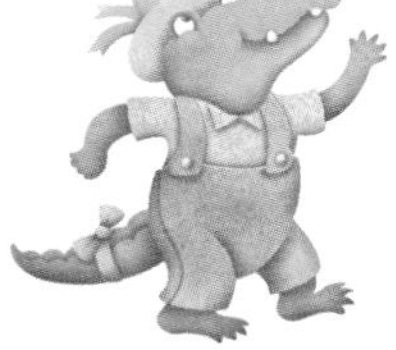

I am Ann.

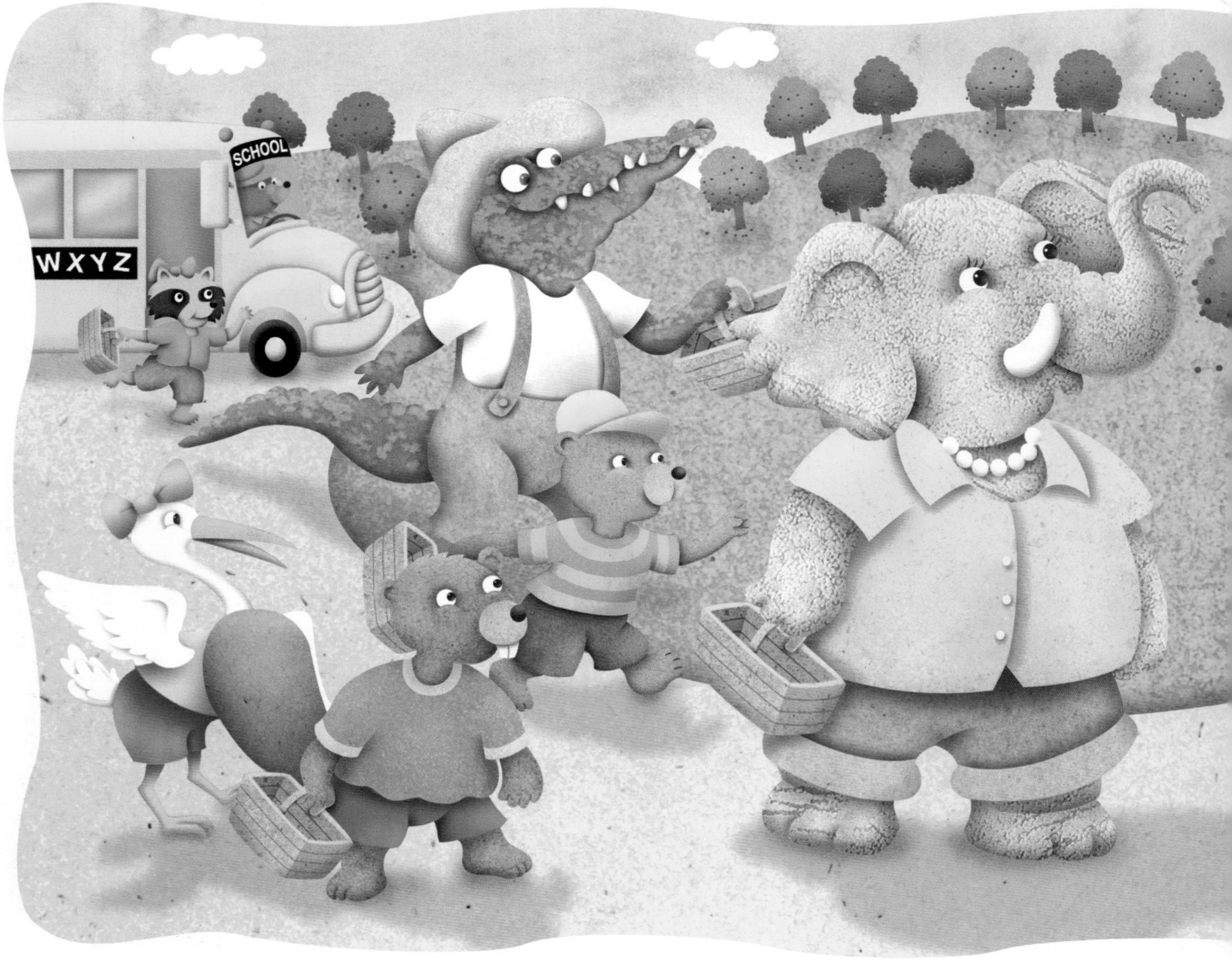

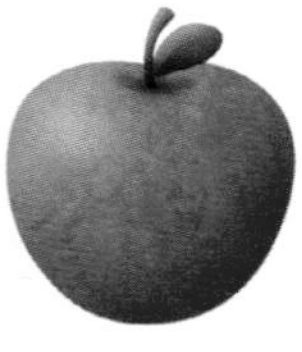

apple

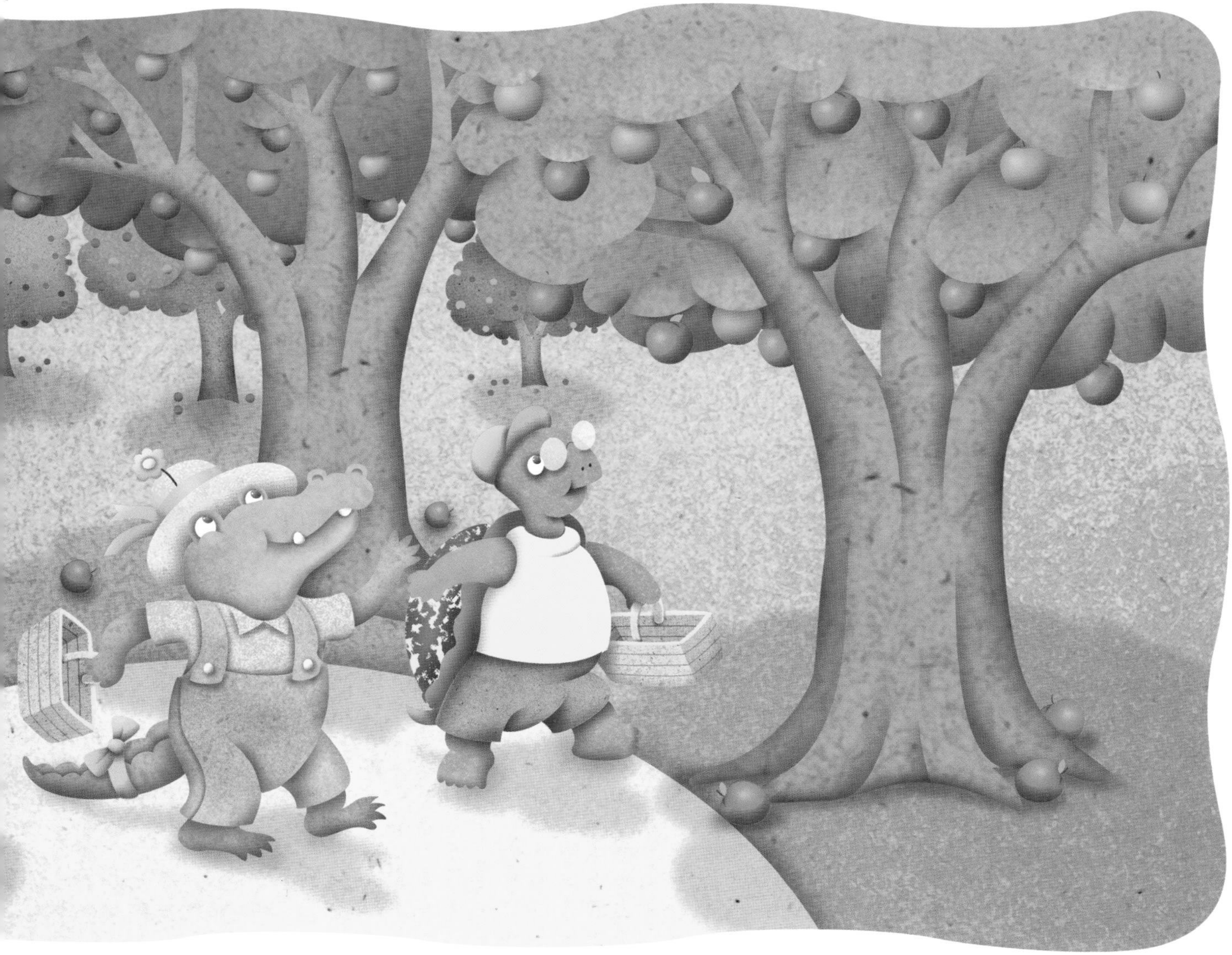

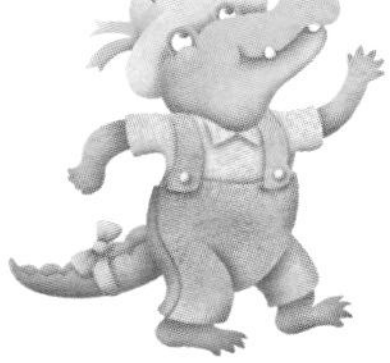

I am Ann.

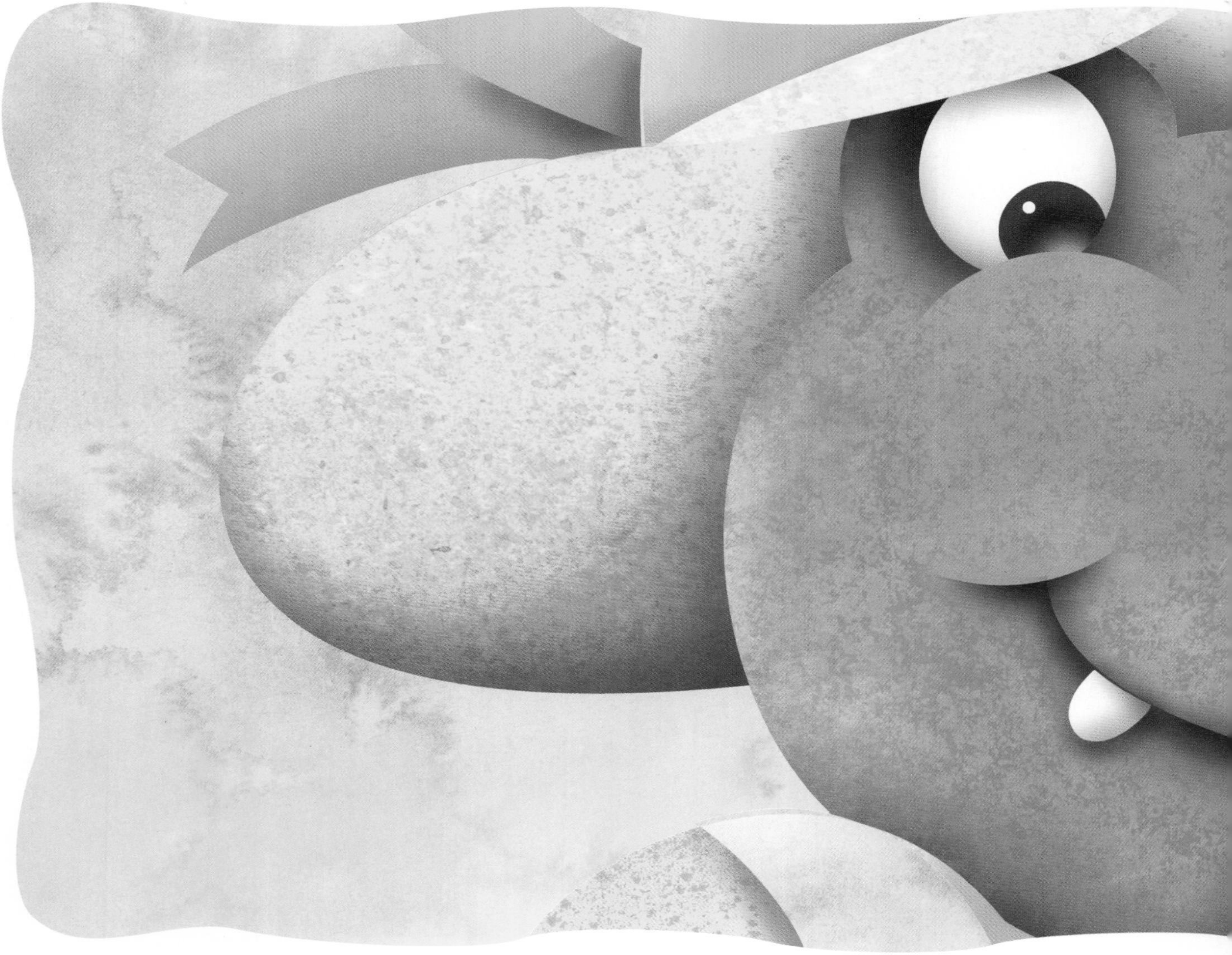

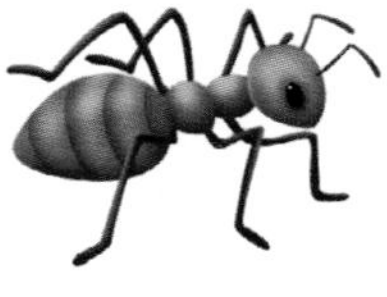

ant

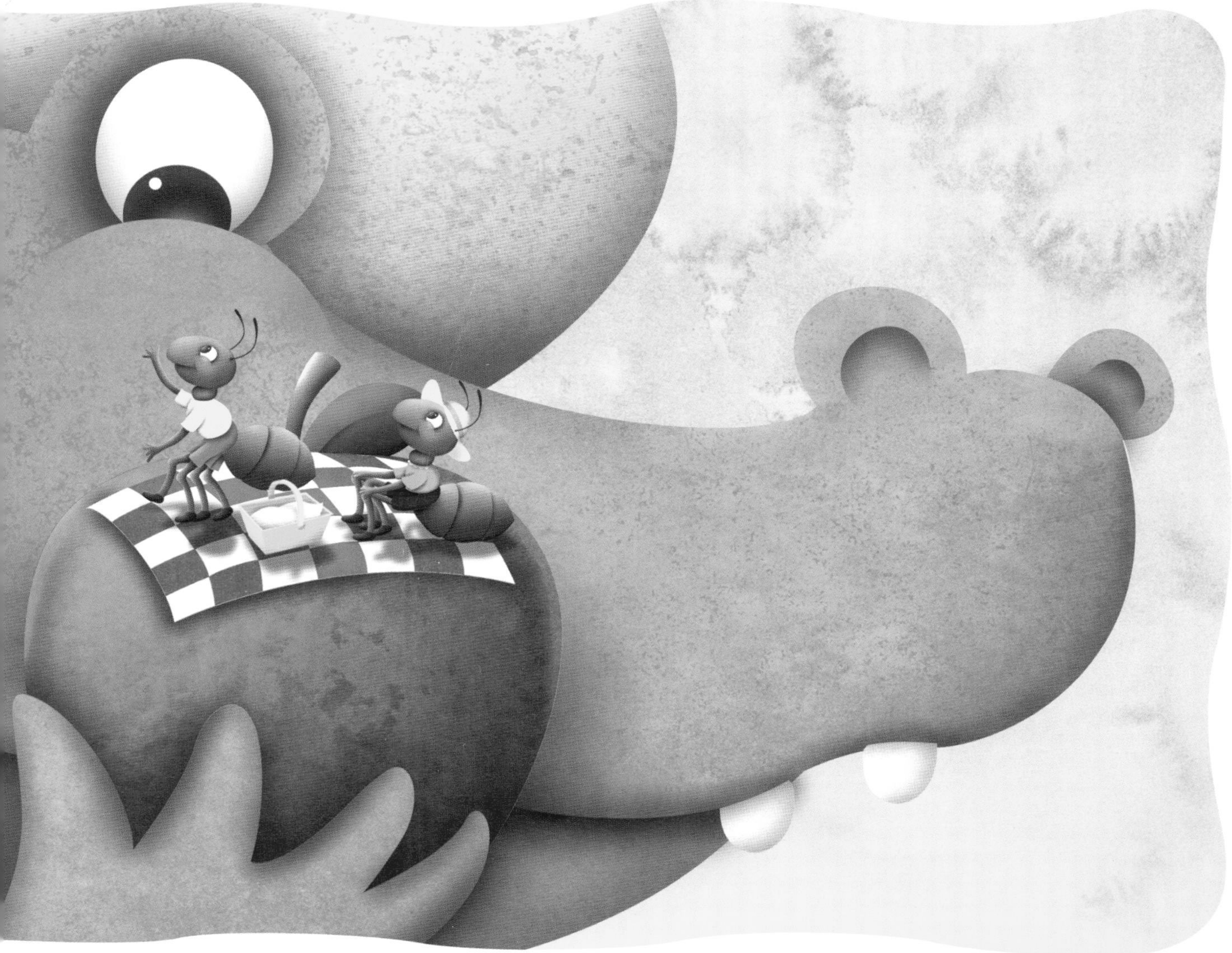

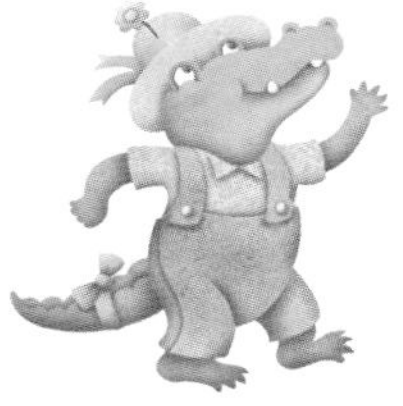

I am Ann.

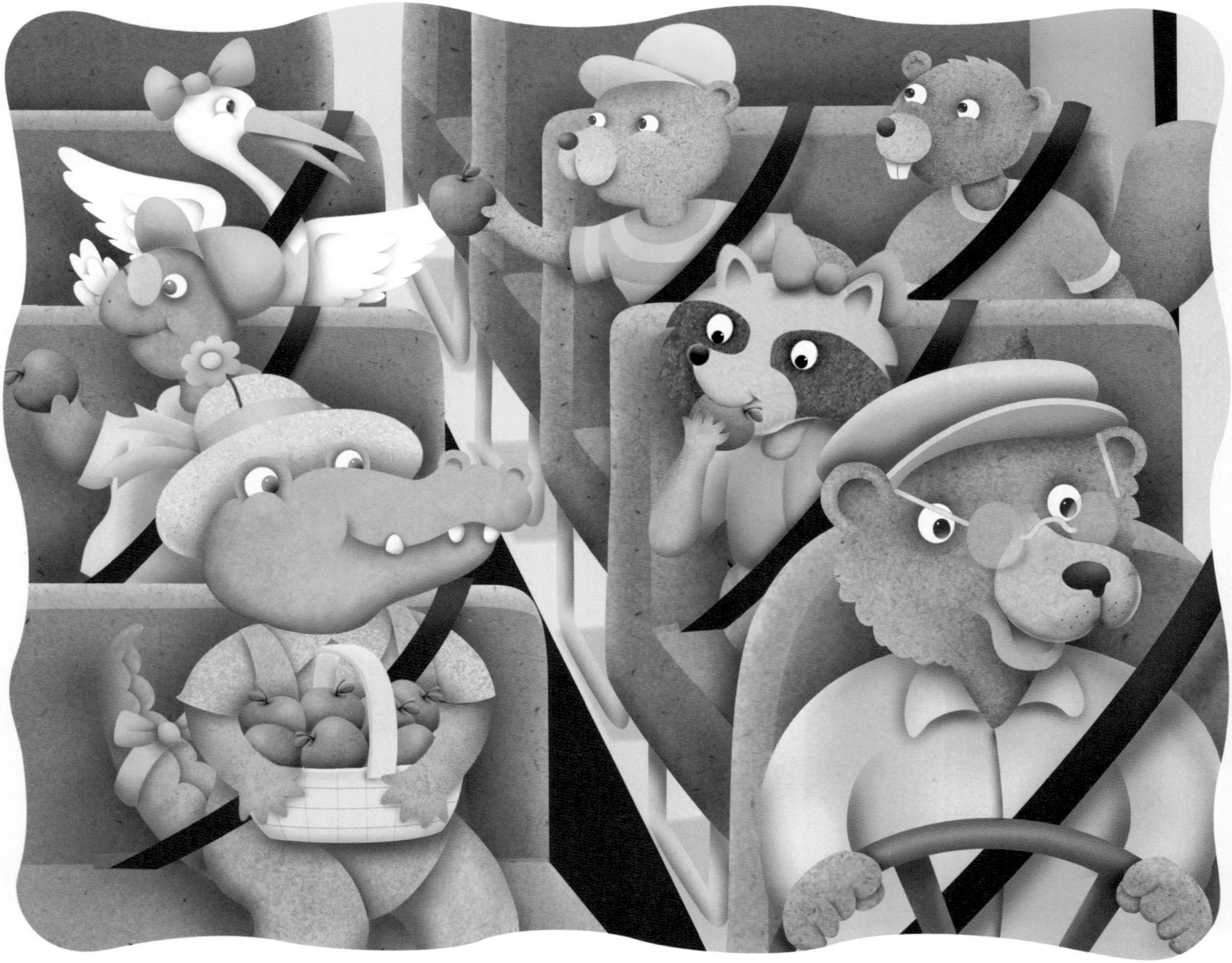

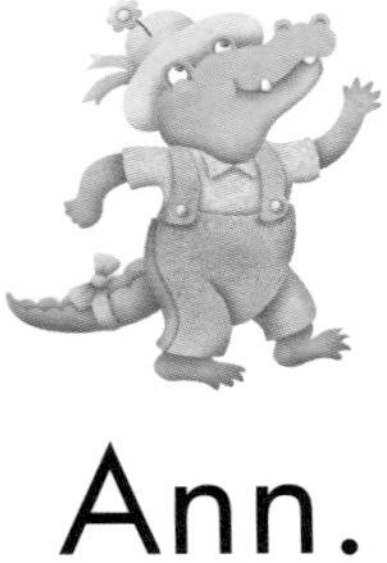

I am Ann.